THE SECRETS TO
HEALTHY
SELF ESTEEM

HOW TO REPAIR AND IMPROVE YOUR SELF-ESTEEM

ALFRED BELLANTI

The Secrets to Healthy Self Esteem: *How to repair and improve your self-esteem*

First Printing: October 2020
Paperback ISBN: 978-0-6489582-1-5
eBook ISBN: 978-0-6489582-0-8

Book Interior and E-book Design by Amit Dey

Follow the blogs and articles on www.howtotreatdepression.org

Disclaimer

Every care has been taken to ensure that the knowledge and techniques in this book are workable and safe. Success using this knowledge and techniques may vary from person to person depending on how well the knowledge is applied and how thoroughly the exercises are done. The book is very helpful but is not intended as a total substitute for consultation with a mental health practitioner.

INTRODUCTION

How do you rate your self-esteem? Can you improve it? Does everyone have self-esteem? How does self-esteem develop? How does childhood trauma or abuse affect self-esteem? Is there a way of bringing up children to have strong self-esteem?

These and many other questions arose while I was researching for informative and helpful content for this book. Read on and these questions shall be answered. Most importantly you will discover how to improve your self-esteem, achieve more of what you want in life and learn what you can do as a parent to bring up your kids to have a healthy self-esteem.

Many people, maybe even you, are lacking self-esteem in some area of life. This lack of esteem could be putting you at risk of not living up to your highest potential, and what could be worse, when the end draws near, you could possibly regret all the things you never achieved because your self-esteem led you to believe you could not.

You are more than you think you are. By reading this book you will discover how your self-esteem or lack of it developed; this will give you a better understanding of yourself. By understanding yourself in a new light and by participating in the techniques and exercises provided in the book your self-esteem will be boosted and you'll be more able to accomplish things in your life that you wanted to achieve but never thought you could.

At the end of my first Senior High School year I failed all High School subjects including English and Literature. My self-esteem went right down and I thought I would never be any good for anything. Now here I am the author of three "Self Help" Books, a Fictional Adventure and a Psychological Thriller. I was able to attain a Bachelor's Degree from University plus several Diplomas and I ran my own Hypnotherapy Practice for more than 25 years until retirement. I'm here to let you know that no matter where you stand right now, you can build or rebuild your self-esteem just like I did.

The material in this book is the result of years of personal life experience and from my Clinical Hypnotherapy Practice. I have also interviewed several people, and researched most of the available literature on the topic so that I can include knowledge from greater minds than mine.

The book is written in an easy going style which should make it a pleasant experience. Therefore enjoy the book and most importantly, do the exercises that have been provided that will help improve your self-esteem. I have great confidence that you can do it! I wish you all the best on your life journey.

WHAT IS IN THIS BOOK

How Do You Rate Your Self-Esteem?

This is an interesting question because during my research someone asked me "What is self-esteem and how do we know we have it?" In the next chapter I shall attempt a definition of 'self-esteem' but I think most readers have a good idea of what it is, so how do we rate it?

My favorite way for self-measurement is the scale from zero to ten. Zero being no self-esteem and ten being the highest self-esteem.

0 1 2 3 4 5 6 7 8 9 10

Interesting things happen when you do this, for example one of my Facebook respondents who at first said she has no self-esteem then said if she does have it would be around 0.000001%. I replied to her "The fact that you responded to my post shows me that you care enough about yourself to ask the question," therefore you do have self-esteem.

A number of people asked me what is the difference between self-esteem and self-confidence. At first it seems that one would be the same as the other but on further thought there could be a difference. For instance you could have high self-confidence but low self-esteem. More about the differences shall be discussed in a later chapter.

So how do you rate your self-esteem? Is it from 0 to 4, at 5, or 6 to 10? If you are happy with your score, that's good. If your score is low and you want to improve it, read on! By the end of this book you will know everything there is to know about self-esteem. You will be presented with exercises you can do to raise your self-esteem and you will get to rate yourself again so you can see your improvement.

The other thing I concluded from my research is that any self-esteem measurement may not remain steady twenty four seven unless you are one hundred percent solid in integrity, which I will talk about later. And self-esteem can increase as your skills in dealing with life events and other people improve.

For a more comprehensive measurement of your self-esteem you may like to use the Rosenberg Scale from the Fetzer Institute -

Instructions

Below is a table with a list of statements dealing with your general feelings about yourself. Please indicate how strongly you agree or disagree with each statement by placing a ✔ in the appropriate column.

Item	Strongly Agree	Agree	Disagree	Strongly Disagree	Score
1. On the whole, I am satisfied with myself					
2. At times I think I am no good at all					
3. I feel I have a number of good qualities					
4. I am able to do things as well as most people					
5. I feel I do not have much to be proud of					
6. I certainly feel useless at times					
7. I feel that I'm a person of worth, at least on equal plane with others					
8. I wish I could have more respect for myself					
9. All in all, I am inclined to think that I am a failure					
10. I take a positive attitude toward myself					

Scoring Instructions: Except for items 2, 5, 6, 8 and 9 which are reverse scored give "Strongly Disagree" one point, "Disagree" two points, "Agree" three points, and "Strongly Agree" four points. Add up scores for all ten items. Higher scores indicate higher self-esteem.

The highest score you can get is 40 and the lowest is 10. The higher the score, the more the self-esteem overall. Then you can also check the score on each individual item, which will give you an indication where you can improve.

What is Self-Esteem?

The concept of self-esteem has its origins in the 18th century, first expressed in the writings of David Hume. This Scottish enlightenment thinker showed the idea that it is important to value and think well of yourself because it serves as a motivational function that enables people to explore their full potential.

It was philosopher, psychologist, geologist, and anthropologist William James (1892) who introduced the term self-esteem as a psychological term.

Now the term self-esteem is used widely as a concept both in popular language and in psychology. It refers to an individual's sense of his or her value or worth, or the extent to which a person values, approves of, appreciates, prizes, or likes him or herself (Blascovich & Tomaka, 1991)

An example of popular use of the concept comes from Gloria Gaynor, a singer and entertainer (I Will Survive,) who said "We all know that self-esteem comes from what you think of you, not what other people think of you." Though this is partly true, it is not the full story.

A more worthwhile definition comes from Rosenberg at the University of Maryland USA - "self-esteem is only one component of the self-concept, which Rosenberg defines as 'totality of the individual's thoughts and feelings with reference to himself or herself as an object.' Besides self-esteem, self-efficacy or mastery, and self-identities are important parts of the self concept."

In some cases self-esteem is described as a feeling, for example "I feel good about myself," or "I feel worthless," "I feel I'm no good for anything."

Although it seems that self-esteem is not a "thinking" thing it is often said that it is thoughts that bring about feelings, whether conscious thoughts or unconscious thoughts. We may not be fully aware of the thoughts or "self talk" that eventually create the feeling. A philosophical discussion about this idea is similar to asking what came first, the chicken or the egg? More about this later.

The real danger with regards to self-esteem is to believe you are the way you are and there is no other way you can be.

Thankfully by now you will have a good idea what self-esteem means to you. At least enough of an idea to be able to work on your own self-esteem.

Whatever your issue is you will discover in this book how and why these thoughts, ideas or beliefs have come into your head, how to overcome them and how to become who you really are once you have freed yourself from these restrictive thoughts or ideas.

I remember being in a band in my late teens. I was in the background just strumming guitar and providing backing vocals. When in private I tried to play lead guitar, I would do a few notes then think, 'This is too hard, I'll never be good enough.' These thoughts were not good for my self-esteem. How wrong I was, because years later I switched to bass guitar, became quite good at it and motivated others to jam with me, I played with bands and created my own band. My Self-esteem went up again, and with regards to playing lead guitar I am doing a course which is greatly improving my skills.

It is **never too late!** Don't let mistaken beliefs about yourself hold you back! Read on, find out how to get to the roots of this problem, understand them, follow the steps to overcome them and start to live the kind of life you have only dreamt of.

Doubting your abilities, believing that somebody else is better than you, or thinking you cannot do a job well, are common examples of low self-esteem. The way you feel about yourself directly affects your personal life, your relationships, and your career. Low self-esteem can also lead to lack of self care, self neglect, self abuse, drug or alcohol addiction or self harm.

A good friend Elizabeth was heavily controlled by her parents. The unfortunate outcome of this for Elizabeth was that she grew up feeling incapable of doing things for herself. In other words her low self-esteem was "put into" her because of parental control. Thankfully Elizabeth is "recovering" from this. Through her participation in the processes explained in this book she is "mending" herself.

Some of the most common characteristics of low self-esteem are:

- Depression / sadness.
- Anxieties.
- Low mood.
- Avoidance of social situations.
- Feelings of inadequacy.
- Comparing self-negatively to others.
- Difficulty accepting compliments.
- Neglect of own needs, particularly emotional ones.

On this last point it can be said that people pleasers typically have low self-esteem. They overdo it on kindness and helpfulness because they feel a need to prove their worth. They're uncomfortable with conflict or negative emotions, so they work hard to always keep their partners or others happy, with no concern for their own feelings.

It has been said that self-esteem is a balance between acceptance and rejection. From this point of view it is easy to see why people pleasers do what they do; it is because they are seeking to be accepted by others.

In her article on bustle.com Teresa Newcombe says "Low self-esteem affects relationships in so many ways that it's almost mind blowing. There are almost too many negative side effects to list. Relationship behaviors that might mean you have low self-esteem are, coincidentally, common fight starters, and even breakup fuel. And because you've probably been battling low self-esteem most of your life, and through all your relationships, you probably don't even notice you're doing these things — or you think they're normal relationship behaviors. They're not."

People with deep insecurities and low self-esteem feel unworthy of love, and scared that they'll lose it at any moment. This can lead to clingy behavior, as you try too hard to hold on to something you're afraid to lose.

It can also mean you're letting your relationship take up your identity, so you don't know what to do with yourself when you're alone.

Co-dependence often happens when both partners have low self-esteem. It's when you depend on each other too much. It can look like never going anywhere without each other, feeling unable to live without each other, or setting up your lives so they don't work unless you're together. People with healthy self-esteem maintain their individual identities and most of their independence.

Some of the many causes of low self-esteem may include: Unhappy childhood where parents (or other significant people such as teachers) were extremely critical. Poor academic performance in school resulting in a lack of confidence. Ongoing stressful life events such as relationship breakdown or financial trouble.

Poor academic performance wrecked my self-esteem back in the days when I was transferred to a school where the academic standard was much higher than my previous school - I failed the final year exams. It wasn't until several years later that I recovered my self-esteem after passing the equivalent exams at an adult college. This gained me admission to university.

Understanding the mechanisms by which these life events affect our brain and create seemingly irreparable neural connections will help you to undo the mecha-nisms and lead you to living a better life. You will learn later in this book how to repair or improve your self-esteem. For now, keep reading more about the topic because as they say, "better the devil you know than the devil you don't know."

How Does Self-Esteem Develop?

I n his monumental work "The Six Pillars of self-esteem" Nathaniel Branden tells us that self-esteem is created from external factors as well as internal factors.

Studies of young children show clearly that parents' style of child rearing during the first three or four years determines the amount of self-esteem that a child starts with.

As soon as babies are born, they begin to learn about the world. It is from these early experiences, and from what they see, hear and feel within the family, that they start to develop ideas about themselves. They learn whether they are loved, valued and belong, and whether they are okay or not.

Self-esteem issues can develop later in life too, as was the case with Elizabeth whom you met previously in this book. Elizabeth grew up in a loving family. Her dad worked long hours and was very tired when he got home. Mom worked nights, so Dad was the main caregiver to Elizabeth and her brother Bill as youngsters.

Unfortunately Elizabeth came under further parental control, namely her dad, because she became pregnant, the baby's father abandoned them, and she had to move back home. Her self-esteem hit rock bottom.

But what about before babies are born? Is there any factor in heredity that may play a role? Dr. Shelley E. Taylor and Shimon Saphire-Bernstein of the University of California, Los Angeles, and their colleagues set out to determine if certain variants of the OXTR gene, which codes for oxytocin receptors, played a role in development of optimism, self-esteem and personal mastery.

The study was done by comparing questionnaire answers of 326 volunteers with analysis of their DNA. The comparison showed that volunteers with a particular gene variant were less optimistic, had lower self-esteem and felt less personal mastery than people with the other variant.

After presenting the findings Dr Taylor concluded by saying "Some people think genes are destiny, that if you have a specific gene, then you will have a particular outcome. That is definitely not the case," This gene is one factor that influences psychological resources and depression, but there is plenty of room for environmental factors as well."

Another determinant in the development of self-esteem is school. One of the best ways to improve confidence is to engage kids in various self-esteem activities for students. By boosting self-esteem in students, children who may come from less than desirable home settings can learn skills that foster a sense of community and respect. Students' self-esteem is directly related to their school performance. By ensuring that student self-esteem is healthy, the environment for learning becomes one where education and learning thrives. Self-esteem activities for students are an excellent way to help boost a child's confidence and increase learning. Many self-esteem activities for students can be used including those that are used in an individual as well as classroom setting.

The major cause of poor self-esteem is past negative programming that is the product of judgmental parents. Say for example a boy takes seventeen units at school and gets four B's and one C but no A's, the parent says "your grades are bad." Or a girl who plays soccer and doesn't score any goals but makes a clever move that placed the ball at the foot of a team member who kicks the winning goal gets called a lousy player because it wasn't her that scored the goal. Constant criticisms such as these do not help to develop healthy self-esteem.

Self-esteem can be affected by certain life events too. For example a sensitive person makes a mistake at work and the boss shouts at him calling him stupid and incompetent. This sensitive person could easily develop low self-esteem as a result.

Self-esteem can decrease or increase depending on what is happening to you or around you. This is called situational self-esteem. Only a very evolved person can keep self-esteem steady all life through. It is possible to reach that state through regular meditation and this is what I do, I practice Vedic Meditation.

Self-esteem may suffer from the way you perceive yourself. I remember a case where a primary grade school student who was overweight was brought out in front of her class by her teacher who also happened to be a Weight Watchers promoter.

The teacher held a picture of herself and, pointing at the pupil, said "who would you rather look like? Her or me?" What an awful thing that happened to that poor child. It is no wonder that her self-esteem plummeted to the ground.

I recently interviewed a friend about self-esteem. He is studying for a Masters in Teaching. He explained how his self-esteem slumped when he spent too much time in his comfort zone, not doing much. When I asked him why, he said he felt non-productive.

I asked him what he did to send his self-esteem back up. He said that firstly he went to the gym, which increased his serotonin and dopamine levels, then went back to his course work which made him feel better about himself. More about raising your self-esteem will be revealed later in this book.

Last but not least, I must make reference to readers from cultural backgrounds or religions that believe in reincarnation. And the question here is can levels of self-esteem come about as a result of good or bad karma from a previous life?

If you think or feel that your self-esteem needs repair and improvement read on. The more you know about self-esteem the more easily you will be able to improve it.

The Inner Critic

first came across this term "The Inner Critic" in the early days of my practice when clients presented with low self-esteem. I have to admit I didn't know enough to be of great help so I bought a book about self-esteem by Matthew McKay PhD and Patrick Fanning.

The first term used in the book was "The Pathological Critic" a term originally coined by psychologist Eugene Sagan to describe the negative inner voice that attacks and judges you. Everyone has a critical inner voice. But people with low self-esteem tend to have a more vicious and vocal pathological critic. Later in the book this term mellowed to "internal critic," then "inner critic."

This inner critic blames you for things that go wrong, compares you to others' achievements and abilities, and finds you wanting. It sets impossible standards of perfection then beats you up for the smallest mistake.

The critic remembers all your failures but never once reminds you of your strengths or accomplishments. It tells you to be the best, and if you're not the best, you're nothing. It calls you names - stupid, incompetent, ugly, selfish, weak - and makes you believe that all of them are true.

In chapter 2 we touched on the concept that self-esteem is the result of conscious or unconscious thought. Thought in this context can be considered to be the voice of your inner critic. This voice is so insidious, so much ingrained as part of your brain that you never notice its devastating effect. It becomes so much a part of you that it seems natural to believe that you are the way you are and that's it; you can't be any other way.

Can you think of any thought or criticism about yourself that affected you at any stage of your life? I can, and the revelation occurred to me just now. During my career as a hypnotherapist I often had to take on casual or part time jobs to cover the cost of maintaining my practice.

One such job was in a shop that sold cell phones, I was in the back office doing admin work. When asked to go and help in the shop I felt stupid and incompetent, but why?

I realise only now that in early high school days we were sent to sit for some aptitude tests which revealed I had a low understanding of technical or mechanical workings. And I remember how I was convinced that I could not get involved in selling phones because I could not understand the technology enough to be able to deal with questions that customers may ask. Now I realise that the root of this self limiting belief was the result of that test fifty years before.

I could have easily overcome that belief by learning enough about the technology to become more confident in the face of customers.

Take a few moments now to reflect on any limiting thoughts or beliefs about yourself, try to work out how or why they occurred, and ponder or think about a way to overcome this 'damage' to your self-esteem. Later in the book you will be guided on ways to do this but the best way could be your way of doing it, and you could end up writing your own book.

Do not make the same mistakes I did. You risk not only making your life miserable but you rob yourself of the success that could be rightfully yours. Why do this, when you can learn to help yourself repair and improve your self-esteem.

A few years ago I came across a wonderful system that helped you discover your particular inner genius. It was based on a simple principle of discovering in which area your genius lies.

Just as you wouldn't expect a fish to climb a tree or a bird to live in a fishbowl, your genius would not thrive if you didn't know which circumstances in life would help you thrive. Discussion about this system and application of it goes beyond the scope of this book but read on because you will be guided on how to improve your self-esteem. Once your self-esteem has reached a level that is acceptable to you, it will be time to move on to bigger and better achievements.

Discovering Your Inner Critic

As mentioned before your inner critic is not always obvious to you, it can hide as lack of confidence, nervousness, or as a feeling you are not good enough. It will take some work to bring this critic out of the woodwork so that you can deal with it, crush it, and get rid of it once and for all!

Each moment in your life when you are awake there is self talk going on within, even though you may not be aware of it. You are interpreting your experience, solving problems, thinking about the future or past events. Most of this self talk is useful, but somewhere in this continuous inner dialogue the critic can lurk.

Your job is to become aware of this inner dialogue, "hear" it, and uncover the negative talk. When you have it in your grasp, you will be in a better position to banish it from your life.

In their book about self-esteem McKay and Fanning give an example from a therapy session. You can use this example to help you.

The therapist asked the client what he was thinking during a recent episode of self reproach, then he pointed out the "inner critic" and encouraged the client to develop his own name for this critic. Typical names are "the bully," "the shark," "my kicker," "the wimp," "Mr. Perfect," "Mary" (the client's mother), and so on.

By giving the critic a personality you can externalize this accusing voice. You can experience the voice as something coming from outside, rather than as part of your normal flow of thought.

You can also begin to identify the healthy thoughts and distinguish them from the negative ones. You can call them "my rational part," "my accepting part," "my healthy coach," and so on. You then confront your inner critic. The examples below can be used as a guide:

> Therapist: *So what did the critic say when you waited and didn't hear from your new friend?*
>
> Client: *That I'm not interesting, that I bored him and he was tired of me.*
>
> Therapist: *What does the healthy coach say back to that?*

Client: *That our conversation was lively and fun. That there was nice energy between us. I could feel it*

Therapist: *What else? Does the coach think you should stew about it, or is there some action you can take?*

Client: *I could call him and try to get a sense of how he feels.*

Here's another example:

Client: *I didn't do an assignment at work in time.*

Therapist: *What did the bully say about that?*

Client: *That I'm lazy. Over and over: "You're lazy, you screw up, you'll never get anywhere."*

Therapist: *Can you mobilize the healthy voice to say anything back?*

Client: *All I can hear is the bully.*

Therapist: *Right now see if you can find your healthy voice so you can talk back to the bully. Are you really lazy and a screw up?*

Client: Well, my healthy voice says, *"You did drag your feet, but you still finished it, you turned it in. No one really cared that it was late but you."*

Therapist: *So the bully exaggerated about you screwing up?*

Client: *Yes, he always exaggerates.*

This process is called "Cognitive Restructuring" and the next step is to become aware of the positive function your inner critic serves. I know this can seem hard to believe but there is a positive aspect, can you guess what it is?

Yes! It's positive function is to promote desired behavior, to protect your self worth, or to control painful feelings. This next example will show you how:

Therapist: *When you were feeling nervous during dinner, what was the critic saying?*

Client: *She won't like you. You don't know anything and haven't much money. And you're not very funny.*

Therapist: *Remember we said the critic always tries to meet some need. What was he trying to protect you from this time?*

Client: *By expecting it, then not getting so hurt.*

Therapist: *So the critic was sort of desensitizing you, preparing you. You wouldn't feel quite so bad if she didn't like you because you expect her not to. That's something we've seen a lot of before. It's one of the main functions of your critic - protecting you from the fear of rejection.*

Here you can see that your critic is being reinforced because it gets the reward of being your protector. Now that you realize that, you can become more aware of the inner critic's way to deal with the fear of rejection, or failure, or fear of painful feelings and so on. You can devise better strategies, like this one:

Therapist: *Is there another way of lowering your anxiety about rejection? A way that doesn't use the critic.*

Client: *I guess so. I could remind myself that we're both probably nervous. And that we're just there to have a pleasant evening and it doesn't have to be much beyond that.*

Therapist: *In other words, tell yourself that it's just a date, and you don't necessarily expect her to like you so much that she'll spend the rest of her life with you.*

Client: *Right.*

> Therapist: *Does reframing it like that lower your anxiety.*
>
> Client: *I think so.*

McKay and Fanning identify nine specific categories of distorted thinking that contribute to lower self-esteem. They say that these 'cognitive distortions' are actually bad habits. Habits of thought that you continually use to interpret reality in an unreal way.

Let's say that you invite a friend over to your house and she replies *"sorry I can't, I have too much to do today."* You could just accept that she is very busy or you can default to your habit of thinking about any type of rejection as a personal insult, thereby again attacking your self-esteem.

Distorted thinking styles (cognitive distortions) cause you to see the world in a distorted way, as though your view of the world is the only reality, which in fact it isn't. Please note that not all of these apply to you personally. They are presented here to make a point, and these are not accusations, they are here for educational purposes. The distortions are categorized as follows:

1. **Overgeneralization** - From one isolated event you make a general, universal rule. For example - If you fail once, you will always fail.

2. **Global Labelling** - You automatically use down-grading labels to describe yourself, rather than accurately describing your qualities.

3. **Filtering** - You pay more attention to the negative and disregard the positive.

4. **Polarized Thinking** - You lump things into absolute black and white categories with no shades of grey, e.g. you have to be perfect or you're worthless.

5. **Self-Blame** - You consistently blame yourself for things that may not really be your fault.

6. **Personalization** - You assume that everything has something to do with you, and you negatively compare yourself to everyone else.

7. **Mind Reading** - You assume that others don't like you, are angry with you, don't care about you, and so on, without any real evidence that your assumptions are correct.

8. **Control Fallacies** - You either feel that you have total responsibility for everyone and everything, or feel that you have no control, that you're a helpless victim.

9. **Emotional Reasoning** - You assume that things are the way you feel about them.

Shut Up Your Critic or Not

*"W*ould you rather look like her"* said the teacher pointing to Helen, the nine year old obese girl whom she had ordered to stand in front of the class, *"or would you rather look like this?"* pointing to a picture of her own perfect body. A horrible experience for Helen, you must admit.

You can imagine the effect that would have had on a nine year old. Her self-esteem would have been damaged for a long, long time. Everytime she looked in the mirror she would see herself as obese, ugly and undesirable. The result of an inner voice which was not even her own voice to start with.

You may or may not have an experience of negative body image that affects your self-esteem. If you have, your inner critic could be saying *"I don't like the look of my body, I'm too fat!" "I wish I was slimmer", "why can't I look like Jillian down the road?"*

Now that you know more about your inner critic and how it operates, you have to think about how to shut its mouth or at least get it to give you some more positive criticism. Positive criticism won't be given to you directly by the way, you'll have to think for yourself and find the 'healthy voice' as previously mentioned.

In the case of body image aren't you indirectly being told to do something about your weight? Eat healthier food? Exercise? Diet? Or whatever?

Remember that there is always a good intention there, believe it. The critic is trying to remind you that you could be better, do better, or think in a different way so there's no need to shut it up, you can ally with it and get it to help you. Let me give you some examples that involve different scenarios:

Work Situation: Inner critic - *"I never get my projects done in time."* What do you think it's telling you? Is it possibly hinting that you should maybe manage your time better? Work a little faster?

Relationships: Inner critic - *"She doesn't understand me."* Is your critic perhaps telling you that you're not explaining yourself clearly enough? Maybe you're using the wrong words? The wrong voice tone?

Social Situation: - Inner critic - *"No one talks to me at parties,"* *"They always ignore me."* Now this is something I can really tell you about, because many years ago I used to go to parties that a friend told me about. I turned up at parties where I knew no one but my friend wasn't there, so I just stood back against a wall feeling ignored and wondering why no one took notice of me. It wasn't until many years later that I realised it was me who was at fault. If I had only intro-duced myself to people instead of standing back the outcome would have been different. What is your take on this?

Before I started to write this book I interviewed a num-ber of people and I'm glad I did. Interviewing people who have experienced self-esteem problems has given me more insight to share with you so that you can ben-efit from their experiences. And later in the book you will be provided with strategies that will help you achieve healthy self-esteem, a bonus on top of what you have learned already.

People are different in many ways but there are a lot of similarities in the workings of the mind.

One of the ways that your "inner critic" can harass you is by getting you to think *"I should do this"*, *"I shoulda done that"* and so on.

This is what Elizabeth has to say: *"When I'm down and I know my dirty laundry is piling up, my room is in a mess and I can't find anything, I compare myself to my*

sister who is so organized. This is when the 'shoulds'
come in. 'I should do this', 'I should do that'."

I will write more about the 'shoulds' in another chapter.
For now, let me tell you something else that Elizabeth
told me: *"Once I was getting ready to go to a party.*
I went to my wardrobe and realized I had no clean
clothes to wear. I stomped around the house shouting
angrily ' F . . k! I shoulda done my washing!' Dad heard
me and shouted back 'that's typical you - shoulda done
this, shoulda done that, but nothing gets done!' "

Convert Your Critic
into Your Ally

I n a previous chapter you were introduced to the concept of giving your inner critic a name and a voice. You were also told that there is a part of you that is more positive, and you can call that your 'healthy critic.'

The previous chapter talked about how your inner critic has a positive intent. For example when your inner critic says "you are lazy" you can interpret that voice as a hint to get doing something, finish a project, or whatever. Take this scenario for instance:

Joan wants to paint her room, she has moved most of the furniture away from the walls and covered it and all that's left to do now is to apply the paint. She is dragging her feet and just doesn't feel like doing it. her inner dialogue runs something like this:

"Come on Joan, you know you want this room painted and fresh!"

"But I don't feel like doing it!"

"Joan, you're so lazy!"

Now take the same scenario and reframe the ending - *"Joan, you're so lazy!"* When her "inner critic" says that, what else is it telling here indirectly? This is where her self therapy comes in, it will take some self-training but the result will be well worth it. This is an example of self therapy:

"Joan, you're so lazy!"

Here Joan can pause for a moment and think. *What is the positive side of this statement?*

"Ah, it's reminding me of the past, when I was too lazy to finish a job. Now I'll get on with it, paint the room, and I'll feel much better for it!"

Here Joan has succeeded in turning her inner critic into an ally. Can you come up with any negative statements that your "inner critic" is throwing at you? Dive within for a few moments and find some. Then think about how you can recruit that critic to become your ally.

In the first column of the table below you write critical statements that you have experienced. In the second column, write a positive reframe. The first few lines of the table have been filled as examples:

Inner Critic Voice	Positive Reframe
You're so fat	I've been like this too long now, it's time I do something about it.
I look so daggy	Tired of looking like this, it's time for a makeover
You're a terrible cook	That's right, I could do with a few cooking lessons or Google some recipes with easy instructions

If you need, you can draw a table like this one and fill it yourself. Write the positive reframes and remember them if you can, or keep the table handy to refer to when you want. Please note that it is not engraved in stone and you can amend, adjust, modify or rewrite it at any time.

This is just one of the tasks for you to complete to help you raise your self-esteem. Hopefully you're not afraid of hard work because there will be more tasks and exercises for you to do as this book evolves. As far as I know, no one has ever written about self-esteem quite in this way.

Another thing for you to think about are your personal values. Everyone has within them a value system. It could be your own or the values could have been imposed upon you through your upbringing. Dare I say that even if you think or feel you have no inner values, that can be of value in itself.

Firstly, what is a value? Wikipedia says:

"In ethics, value denotes the degree of importance of some thing or action, with the aim of determining what actions are best to do or what way is best to live, or to describe the significance of different actions."

So if you were brought up to be strictly religious, you are likely to hold religion as being important in your life.

If your parents followed a particular football team, it is likely that you follow that team too, and would like that team to win, because you value the team.

How Your Values Can Cause
Low Self-Esteem

This exercise, borrowed from Michael Yapko's "Breaking from the Patterns of Depression" will help you improve your self-esteem by recognizing that every part of you is valuable at some place at some time, and even the parts of you that you had not liked before may make useful contributions to your life within the right context.

Yapko tells us of a patient, Emma, who described herself as gentle, kind, and considerate most of the time but occasionally became enraged for no apparent reason, putting her family in danger by throwing things or getting violent with them.

Emma grew up with parents who placed strong value on her being sweet and good, but they devalued her expression of the other basic emotions, namely anger. They used to tell her "if you have nothing nice to say, or if you can't be pleasant, say nothing!"

As a result Emma took part of herself, her angry feelings, and labelled them "bad" and spent a lot of time and energy suppressing them no matter what the situation was. And you know what happens in a volcano when lava pressure builds up to critical level do you not?

Can you guess what Emma feels about herself when she erupts? Especially when she endangers her family? That's right - she feels self hatred, despair and depression.

Yapko states that when you suppress basic and natural parts of yourself as "bad" it is a strategy that's bound to fail. For example trying to eliminate an appetite for sweets can lead to eating binges, trying to suppress normal sexual feelings can lead to acting out those feelings in a sexually irresponsible way.

Emma did not realise that there are times when expressing anger verbally is OK. Anger can sometimes serve a positive outcome, for instance defending herself against unfair criticism, defending others against unfairness, or for setting appropriate limits and boundaries with others.

The same with Elizabeth from an earlier chapter. Elizabeth didn't like the part of her that is unable to stand up for herself. Her father had always told her what to do and put her down all the time. This happened even when she wanted to do things that were good for her like going to the gym. Once she identified those parts, and followed the self-therapy steps given in this book she was able to live a more fulfilled life.

In the table below, list the 'parts' or characteristics of yourself that you normally think of as 'bad' or negative. Now generate at least three examples of specific situations where those parts have positive values.

What this important exercise illustrates is that with most problems, if you employ the 'wrong' part of you for the context; it is not the outcome of personal weakness or disease. It has more to do with past conditioning. Use the outline and examples in the table to help you get started.

My 'Bad' Part	Places It Can Have Positive Value
Anger	Defending myself against unfair criticism Defending others against unfairness Setting appropriate limits with others
Competitive-ness	Challenging myself to improve in an area Playing on a sports team Striving to improve a better product or service in order to succeed in business

Fill in the rest of the table above and if you need, make your own list.

Values are something that you grew up with, they came from your parents, your teachers, your church, your peers, the media and possible other sources. Maybe it's time to examine your values.

Do you value:

- Freedom more than discipline?
- Self expression more than conformity?
- Leisure more than hard work?
- Activity more than rest?
- Sexual freedom over chastity?
- Religion more than atheism
- Nightlife more than early to bed

These are the kinds of questions to explore. Ask yourself, are you living according to your own values or are you living to other values, imposed or taught to you by others?

Self-esteem can suffer when you are trying to live with outdated values. An example from my life was when I failed my exams in the first year of senior highschool. The drop in self-esteem was the result of not having lived up to the high value my mum and dad placed on success at school. Later in life I read about individuals who had become successful with little or no education at all. It made me realize that the values imposed on me by my parents did not hold as true in the modern world where people with little or no education create successful lives for themselves.

So are you trying to live up to values that no longer hold in this day and age? Values that you try to live by but fail, thereby affecting your self-esteem?

Another question I get asked is can external objects such as a flashy car or a luxurious home contribute to healthy self-esteem. In other words is high self-esteem the result of having these, or is it the having of these things that give the owner high self-esteem. This question can be answered in terms of values as explained above. If your set of values include ownership of external and luxurious external objects and you are comfortable with that, then yes these can contribute to healthy self-esteem. For you they could represent achievement.

You may wish to ask yourself - "How would my self-esteem fare if I lost all these things, or they were taken away?"

Core Beliefs

Some of the material in this chapter comes from an article by Andrew Shorten on the website thelawofattraction.com, to which the credit is due. I have included it here for educational purposes.

What Are Core Beliefs And How Do We Form Them?

Core beliefs are our mental foundation which influences all of our actions and experiences in the world. They guide our behaviors on a daily basis with each interaction and each thought. Our core beliefs are essentially responsible for the outcome of our lives.

As I discussed in a previous chapter, core beliefs are formed from various experiences both internally, and externally. This includes things we're told, things we've thought, and things we've learned.

The beliefs could have come from our parents, our school, our church, our friends, the media and just about from anywhere else. Some of us blindly follow beliefs told to us from these institutions. Some of us blindly follow what our parents believe. We also follow the beliefs told to us by our friends and even what we see on Facebook, Instagram, Tik Tok or TV. So you need to ask yourself *where do my thoughts really come from? Are they born out of those beliefs? Am I really thinking for myself, or is my thinking the result of beliefs from elsewhere?*

Once you realize that the negative thoughts or beliefs you hold about yourself most likely did not originate from you, you will get a sense of comfort and relief because it will empower you to change them.

Let's have a look at some examples of negative core beliefs about yourself that might be holding you back from living a really great life:

1. I am worthless
2. I'm not smart
3. I am just not good enough

4. I am a failure
5. I'm a loser
6. I am lazy and unmotivated
7. I'll never get out of debt

Then there could be negative core beliefs about the world that restrict you too:

1. Life is unfair
2. People are generally bad
3. Don't trust anyone
4. Politicians are all corrupt
5. The world is against me

These common core beliefs can disempower you and lead you to feel you have no control over your life. Not only that, you become primed to look for proof that those beliefs are true. There is a tendency to over-look all the positive events in your life and filter only the events that back up your beliefs, giving you a very unbalanced view of yourself and the world.

At this stage you could make a list of your core beliefs so that you can analyse them and find a way that you can 'turn them around.' You will be guided on how to do this later in this book.

To put things into proper perspective you are also provided with some examples of positive core beliefs:

1. I am capable
2. I feel confident
3. I believe in myself and my abilities
4. Life isn't perfect, but it's still great
5. No matter what's happening, there is still so much to be grateful for
6. My happiness is dependent on me, my thinking, and nobody else
7. I take personal responsibility for my mistakes
8. What other people think about me is none of my business
9. I love who I am

It is important that you do not 'beat yourself up' if you don't yet have these positive core beliefs. You will soon learn how to acquire them.

As a matter of fact you can try this exercise right now. In the first column of the table below make a list of negative core beliefs that you have at this present time. Then in the last column a list of what core belief you would like to have in its place. Be positive about this but not unrealistic. Leave the middle column blank for the time being. You'll come back to it after I have filled in some examples to get you started.

Negative Core Belief	Transition Phase	Positive Core Belief
I'm not smart		I am smarter than I believe
I'll never get out of debt		I manage my money better so that I become debt free

These are the instructions:

1. Fill as much as you can in the first and last columns.

2. In the middle column write what you need to do, think or believe in order to make the item in column 3 come true.

3. DON'T LOOK NOW! But below there is an example of the transition phase for the two cases given above. Again DON"T LOOK NOW because you will be robbing yourself of the most important process of this exercise!

Negative Core Belief	Transition Phase	Positive Core Belief
I'm not smart	I pick an interest in my life that I like and become very knowledgeable about it	I am smarter than I believe
I'll never get out of debt	I design a budget that will allow for steady regular repayment of debt until I am debt free. If I can't do the budget myself I shall ask someone to do it with me	I manage my money better so that I become debt free

So far we have been examining self-esteem from a scientific viewpoint. For those of you who believe in God or some Higher Power turn your thoughts upward and realize that this power is on your side and wants the best for you. Nevertheless keep reading just the same.

Some of you may be wondering if there is any medication that can 'treat' low self-esteem. I have looked into this and found that Generalized Anxiety Disorder and other Psychological conditions can be associated with low self-esteem. If you suspect this applies to you you could discuss it with a licenced health professional who may then prescribe an antidepressant or a tranquiliser in addition to some other therapy.

Another exercise you can do is work backward i.e. Start with writing in the first column a positive core belief that you would like to have and then in the second column write what you can do to make that happen. I shall start with two examples from the list shown a few pages back.

Desired Core Belief	What I must do,think or believe to make it come true
I believe in myself and my abilities	It is impossible that I have no abilities at all therefore I look back at things I have done and believe in myself and my abilities to do those things. I will now do more of those things more often to reinforce my belief in myself and my abilities
No matter what's happening, there is still so much to be grateful for	Every day I make a list of everything I am grateful for, it can be a simple thing like a nice cup of coffee, or a nice sunny day, a person you meet, a warm bed at night. There is so much to be grateful for that the list could be endless. I list at least three things each day

Repairing Self-Esteem After Abuse or Bullying

I often get asked how you regain self-esteem after having been bullied as a child, and maybe later as an adult.

Bullying has been an unpleasant fact of life for a long time, likely since the human race started. In recent years there has been more publicity about this because of some sad cases of suicide said to be the result of being consistently bullyied. There has been a splurge of childrens' books published in an attempt both to stop bullying and to help the victims deal with it.

If you are, or have been, a victim of bullying, first you must realize that the fault or blame lies with the bully and not the victim. It is easy to feel your self-esteem being affected, but internally there are two alternatives you can choose:

1. You can let yourself be absorbed into the feeling of being a victim or

2. You can choose to perceive the situation as it really is! - The person who is bullying you is doing it because of some deficiency in their character, they have low self-esteem so there is something wrong with them, not you! A study conducted with 763 teenage school children has verified this.

By giving in to the 'low self-esteem, been put down feeling' you are actually assisting the bully achieve his or her goal to 'put you down and ridicule you'. However if you decide to rise above the feeling and show no response, you become the **victor** and not the victim!

It could be very hard to do on the spot if you are in a state of shock, but if you do it afterward, it will empower you and help your self-esteem to remain intact!

A close friend told me he was punched by another pupil during his early school days. Instead of retaliating or doing much else, he just looked the aggressor in the eye with an expression that conveyed *so what, do you feel better now?* The bully never went near him again.

Other Examples of Abuse

"My father beat me when he was drunk, and he got drunk a lot. But what does that have to do with my inability to stay in a relationship or make commitments?"

"My father and uncle both sexually abused me from the age of five years old. I lived in terror of these two men for most of my childhood. Even though I've been married three times, I still find it impossible to trust my mate and difficult to tolerate sexual intercouse."

The hard question is how do you mend your self-esteem if you have been physically or sexually abused as a child? This has happened within the church, it happens in homes, it happens elsewhere. The victims of this abuse seem to be suffering in a different way to the victims of bullies, or are they? What about victims of rape? Victims of rape often blame themselves, feel guilty, lose trust in men, their relationships can be affected, and they can become nervous and apprehensive.

Hadley and Staudacher tell us that there are three categories of abuse:

- Physical
- Sexual
- Emotional

On top of those three, the main causes of suffering in victims of sexual abuse are:

1. The hurt caused by the betrayal of trust that the victim had toward the person who abused them.

2. A feeling of anger toward the perpetrator and perhaps also toward self.

3. The feeling of guilt because they had been subject to an act that went against the morals as taught in the religion.

4. The blow to self-esteem, being made to feel powerless, a feeling that could last for a long time.

5. Possible loss of faith in the religion which had innocently believed in.

You can imagine the inner turmoil these unfortunate children had gone through and could still still be going through later in life. Are the perpetrators not bullies, as discussed previously?

Andre Brandt PhD MFT writes in Psychology Today: "Trauma generates emotions, and unless we process these emotions at the time the trauma occurs, they become stuck in our mind and body. Instead of healing from the wounding event, the trauma stays in our body as energy in our unconscious, affecting our life until we uncover it and process it out."

Another way to explain this is at a neurological level. The initial trauma causes changes in our neurochemistry, firstly because of the shock, which can put the body into a state of 'freeze' or numbness. This neurological state could persist from some time.

It has been shown in other studies that therapy which addresses the emotions can bring about positive changes in neurochemistry.

"The healthy flow and processing of distressing emotions, such as anger, sadness, shame, and fear, is essential to healing from childhood trauma as an adult." Says Brandt.

At this stage it is worthwhile to introduce to you the topic of 'Neuroplasticity'. Neuroplasticity is a term used to describe that the brain has the capacity to create new neural connections, and fade older connections.

The key to doing this for yourself is repetition. It has been said that it only takes a few days to create a bad habit and as much as twenty one days to create a good habit. The same applies to habits of thought. Low self-esteem can be the result of a particular way of thinking. By training yourself to think in a different way you can create a new 'neural pathway' to better self-esteem.

It had been previously thought that the brain had a fixed number of brain cells and that once these cells were 'killed' by injury, trauma, excessive stress, alcohol or drugs; they would not regenerate. However after reading Norman Doidge's "The Brain that Changes Itself" I now understand how the natural phenomenon 'Neuroplasticity' can be applied to assist people who are suffering self-esteem issues.

If you were subject to Adverse Childhood Events (ACE) such as neglect or abuse and developed low self-esteem, is it possible to repair and improve self-esteem?

Some psychologists believed that your condition would be harder to treat than those who have not had these experiences. They believed that the hypothalamus of people who had experienced severe ACE was underdeveloped. The hypothalamus, the part of the brain that is involved in emotion.

Now the question arises. If these people were to be placed in a kind and protected environment and agreed to stay there until his condition improved, would development of the hypothalamus resume? Would the hypothalamus "grow" to a "normal" size?

A psychologist friend told me that a certain antidepressant drug was shown to add a very thin layer of cells to the hypothalamus. Is it possible that an environment such as described above could provide the right conditions for this to occur naturally, and without drugs?

A possible solution for you, if you are a victim, is to associate with kind, supportive, loving people and accept any kindness that comes your way. Science has proved that pleasant social interaction can raise endorphins, the "feel good" neurochemicals and this effect can last after the interaction. Most importantly be grateful for everything else that you have been given in life. And given all the evil that is happening in the world - is what happened to you really that bad?

I have great faith that you will overcome and survive this, you will continue your life with greater confidence and ability than before. If you need further convincing, in the chapters that follow you will find some exercises that will help you change your current level of thinking and to improve it. You will start to explore some techniques that have been proven to heal the wounds that caused your self-esteem to suffer.

The Child Within

You are reading this book therefore you are a survivor. You have survived to this present moment in spite of what had been done to you in the past. All that is left to do now is to heal the wounds that you suffered way back then, some of which could be affecting you even now. I am referring to feelings of hurt, anger, fear and shame that may still arise from time to time.

These feelings are normal and they can fulfil useful functions such as making you aware that things are not quite right, or protecting you from perceived danger, or reminding you to not get into certain situations. These feelings are only a problem if you find them interfering in your current life. For example if they prevent you forming lasting relationships, leading a normal social life or if you are fearful of meeting new people, and are afraid to trust anyone.

You may need to question yourself. Are these feelings appropriate now? Are they a result of having been abused? Do I really need to let them affect my life?

It has been said that after abuse we unconsciously build up defences. These could include overeating so that we become less attractive to people. Being unattractive then therefore people won't approach us. Another defence is that we could turn to alcohol or drugs because they make us feel better or numb us. In a lot of cases we just avoid people altogether. Have you built up your own defences? If so what are they? It will help for you to know.

Though they say 'A little knowledge is a dangerous thing' and 'Ignorance is bliss' the right amount of knowledge is very helpful. That is what you are getting here, and you can add your own knowledge to what you are getting.

In her Psychology Today article Andrea Brendt says that the best time to respond to childhood emotional wounds is when the trauma first occurs and we realize the violation it has caused to our sense of self and the emotions that follow. Once we realize that the violation doesn't say anything about us personally and don't attach any negative meaning to it we can let it go.

But emotions like anger and sadness are painful and the process doesn't happen automatically so these emotions may be suppressed instead. This is when

"Inner Child" work can provide relief or healing at the adult level.

There was a resurgence of 'inner child work' during the 'new age' at the turn of the century. The effect that the inner child can have on adult behavior has been documented by Jung, Freud and numerous others. More recently Charles L. Whitfield, MD, wrote *Healing the Child Within*, W. Hugh Missildine offered *Your Inner Child of the Past*, and Buck S. Fonvard wrote *Betrayal of Innocence*. Many studies agree that in order to heal past wounds you need to connect with and heal your inner child.

If you are wary or not confident enough to do this yourself, seek professional help. If you are fine with it, just continue reading.

Getting in touch with your inner child is a lot easier than you may think. All you have to do is to sit in a comfortable spot where you will not be disturbed, take a few deep breaths, relax on the out breath, close your eyes and let the image of a child come into your mind. It's OK if the image doesn't appear straight away, just know it is there, feel your inner child, perhaps you can recall a familiar photograph of yourself and if that doesn't work simply know it's there.

Notice your inner child, what is your inner child wearing, does your inner child look happy or sad? Make friends with your inner child, let your inner child know that he or she is safe, wanted and important. Give yourself some time to do this, about 30 or 40 seconds or as long as you need so that it is acknowledged or felt by your inner child.

You could even ask your inner child some questions such as *"what can I do to make you feel better?"* *"What have you been missing?"* *"What information do you need to give me?"* Wait patiently for the answers, nice and easy does it, listen to your inner child.

If your inner child has nothing to say, that's fine, just enjoy being with him or her take your time, give all the love and care you have, remember your inner child is pure, innocent and loveable, no matter what has happened, It deserves your love, affection and care. Let yourself feel that love, warmth and affection.

Hold your child, let your child know how important and precious he or she is. Acknowledge your inner child's existence, and as you communicate your feelings of love and warmth let the feelings join you together and feel a healing taking place. A healing feeling that flows through you completely; though every bone, every nerve and every muscle. Let yourself feel reconnected with your inner child, whole and in harmony with your mind, body and spirit.

You can do this healing exercise over and over, until the healing becomes long lasting or permanent.

The most important thing is to not give up on yourself, there are other ways you can raise your self-esteem. You probably know that people who are going through depression are also experiencing low self-esteem. One of the techniques used to get them out of depression is to get them engaged into something they do well. So how does this apply to you?

Think back to something you used to do well before your self-esteem was damaged. Was it gardening? Cooking? Drawing? Painting? Playing music? Was it a sport perhaps? Or simply a leisure activity like going to a movie, going to the beach or riding a bicycle.

Research has proved that when you do more of what you are good at, you will feel better about yourself. So plan to do something or more than one thing, involve others in it, get positive feedback and approval, it will help raise your self-esteem.

Having personally gone through periods of depression, inactivity and low self-esteem I can speak from experience. I had some talent but I never explored it or tried to improve on it. Now I play bass guitar with three different groups, they appreciate me and I feel so much better about myself because I feel I have accomplished something. One of the groups has released the first album on which I played.

Whatever you are good at - sewing, woodwork, computers - if you don't use any of these skills for yourself, use them for others, they will appreciate you and their thanks and gratitude will do a lot for your self-esteem.

Take a few moments to reflect on what skills you already possess, something you are good at. Look back at things you did well in the past, find those strengths and then look for a way to apply them for yourself or others. Boost your self-esteem!

How to Bring up Children to
Have Healthy Self-Esteem

Before I started to write this book I asked friends and groups on Facebook what question they had about self-esteem. In response to questions from mums and dads I include a summary of an article from pregnancybirthbaby.org.au Much of this will be fairly obvious but is included here to answer the questions.

Praise and encourage your child - It is very important to praise your child for things they do well and also for achieving small steps along the way. Encourage your kids to try again if they don't get it quite right the first time.

Teachers, family and friends should also encourage and praise kids for their achievements and successes no matter how small they may seem.

Some other ways to increase your child's self-esteem - Improving your child's confidence will boost his or her self-esteem.

Spend more time with your children and show that you are interested in what they are doing. You can set realistic goals for your kids and encourage them to have a go.

Encourage their interests and friendships and make sure they feel like they're being heard and they can make decisions for themselves.

Give them a lot of hugs, smile at them a lot, and let them express their feelings.

Coping with disappointment - You have to learn how to cope with disappointment when your kids cannot get something right or can't get their own way. This is also important for the development of their self-esteem.

Guiding toddlers and preschoolers through these emotions can be difficult, but by learning to cope with their own emotions, they increase their self-esteem.

Confidence at school - When your kids go to school praise them for their individual talents not just for their marks. Focus on their strengths. Make time to listen to your kids about what they are doing at school. If they are being bullied talk to their teachers or get professional help.

TEENAGERS

Teenagers deserve a category of their own. Here I can only tell you about the troublesome ones because I was one myself. The 'good ones' follow societal norms and usually have a happy normal life, with its struggles, trials and tribulations.

The troublesome ones need special handling. It seems that their struggles, trials and tribulations are already taking place deep within and that is why they act out in an aggressive, defiant and resentful manner, resistant to authority. They are easily influenced by their peers and social media and distrustful of mainstream thought and propaganda. It is more important for them to live up to the same values of their peer groups than the more traditional values they learned from their parents and other authority figures. Parents have told me they are hard to deal with because they are at that age where "they know everything." Have you had that experience?

So how do you deal with teenagers? (For parents):

Miss Donna (Montessori Schools) says about children and teenagers that you don't become their friend. She starts when they are three and describes her role as "parenting." She says she will become friends with them when they are twenty five and doing really well as a result of her parenting.

According to parents.au.reachout.com if the low self-esteem is not identified and treated, then it can lead to problems such as:

- relationship troubles or difficulty making friends
- negative moods such as feeling sad, anxious, ashamed or angry
- low motivation
- poor body image
- earlier sexual activity
- drinking alcohol and/or taking drugs to feel better

For Teenagers - From kidshealth.com

What If My Self-Esteem Is Low?

You can do things to feel better about yourself. It's never too late. Here are some tips to raise your self-esteem:

Be with people who treat you well. Some people act in ways that tear you down. Others lift you up by what they say and do. Learn to tell the difference. Choose friends who help you feel OK about yourself. Find people you can be yourself with. Be that type of friend for others.

Say helpful things to yourself. Tune in to the voice in your head. Is it too critical? Are you too hard on yourself? For a few days, write down some of the things you say to yourself. Look over your list. Are these things you'd say to a good friend? If not, rewrite them in a way that's true, fair, and kind. Read your new phrases often. Do it until it's more of a habit to think that way.

Accept what's not perfect. It's always good to do the best you can. But when you think you need to be perfect, you can't feel good about anything less. Accept your best. Let yourself feel good about that. Ask for help if you can't get past a need to be perfect.

Set goals and work toward them. If you want to feel good about yourself, do things that are good for you. Maybe you want to eat a healthier diet, get more fit, or study better. Make a goal. Then make a plan for how to do it. Stick with your plan. Track your progress. Be proud of what you've done so far. Say to yourself, "I've been following my plan to work out every day. I feel good about it. I know I can keep it up."

Focus on what goes well. Are you so used to talking about problems that they're all you see? It's easy to get caught up in what's wrong. But unless you balance it with what's good, it just makes you feel bad. Next time, catch yourself when you complain about yourself or your day. Find something that went well instead.

Give and help. Giving is one of the best ways to build self-esteem. Tutor a classmate, help clean up your neighborhood, walk for a good cause. Help out at home or at school. Make it a habit to be kind and fair. Do things that make you proud of the kind of person you are. When you do things that make a difference (even a small one) your self-esteem will grow. **To parents:** Though I have never been a parent I will offer you some other ideas; take them or leave them. It's up to you:

1. Become their ally - Make them really feel that you are on their side, that you agree with their values and aspirations and you will help them along their life path. Tread carefully! If you try to do this while still trying to get them to conform to your values it could backfire.

2. Outmaneuver them - This will be very challenging for you because you will have to 'see' things from their perspective i.e. put yourself in their shoes in the current time, and not from your memory of what it was like when you were their age. Be mindful that the external world has changed drastically since you were their age. I remember my dear mum listening to a conversation between her grandchildren being completely bewildered and saying "I can't understand a thing they are talking about." Now when you see things from their perspective you still have to be at least one step ahead of them within that perspective. It will be as though you are in a parallel universe.

3. Discipline - I went through childhood and teenage years when physical discipline was considered the norm. It was still acceptable to slap or spank your child at home and being caned at school was the way the teachers disciplined the boys. The current thought about discipline is to reward and encourage good behavior, ignore bad behavior and not to react to bad behavior. The idea of ignoring and not reacting to bad behavior applies if the teenager is behaving that way because he or she is wanting attention. The main flaw I see in this method is that it may not always be obvious if the teenager's behavior is purely attention seeking or a cry for help.

Self-Esteem and Humility

Allan was a brilliant computer engineer. He had designed and installed computer systems for some of the top multinational corporations and was in demand by many corporations both large and small.

You would think that Allan would have an inflated ego and an exaggerated sense of self. Nothing could be farther from the truth!

I met Allan at a BBQ a few months ago, before I started writing this book. He was shy, kept his head down unless I was talking to him. When he spoke his eyes were kindly focused on mine and he had a soft smile on his face.

When I praised his achievements he blushed slightly, lowered his head lightly and chuckled very softly. *"Anyone could do it,"* he replied. He was very humble about his achievements.

So what are we to learn from this? It is obvious from this example that self-esteem and humility have no direct connection with each other. A person can have high self-esteem and still be humble. It does not follow that someone with humility would have a low self-esteem. On the contrary, it is more likely that someone with low self-esteem will brag about his or her achievements in order to gain acceptance and recognition to boost his or her self-esteem. Take the case of Julie for example.

Julie was a twenty three year old woman of average looks who could look quite stunning when she dressed up and applied make up. But the truth was that she did not think very much of herself, she had low self-esteem. The only way she knew how to raise her self-esteem was by the number of men she could attract.

Julie's behavior seemed out of sorts with her core beliefs. She believed she was not attractive enough to be interesting to men so she spent time in bars sipping a drink and waited for men to approach her.

It didn't stop at that; men being men would ply her with drink until Julie was intoxicated enough to lose good judgement and would let men seduce her, some more roughly than others because in her mind she was getting attention. The attention temporarily raised her self-esteem.

When she was sober, her self-esteem would plummet back down again, leading her to repeat the same behavior on other nights.

When Julie met up with her girlfriends, she would brag about her "conquests" with men, again this gave her self-esteem another temporary boost.

It is easy to see that Julie, though having low self-esteem, did not display humility, if anything her behavior implied the opposite. In the above examples two factors relating to self-esteem come into play:

1. Values - These were discussed in a previous chapter, and
2. Core Beliefs - We have covered core beliefs in another chapter.

The opposite question has also been raised - Can you have too much self-esteem? This will be covered in the next chapter.

The Result of Too Little or Too Much Self-Esteem

You may think to yourself 'I have no self-esteem.' This is not the same as having low self-esteem. The truth is that everyone has self-esteem whether it is at a conscious or subconscious level. As explained in an early chapter, self-esteem is something that develops from birth or prior to birth. One client exclaimed - "*I have no self-esteem, and if I have it is at 0.00001%.*"

So what is the effect of having too little self-esteem? This is what is said by the Texas University Counseling and Mental Health Center (CMHC):

Low self-esteem can

- create **anxiety**, **stress**, loneliness, and increase likelihood of **depression**.
- cause problems with friendships and romantic relationships.

- seriously impair academic and job performance.
- lead to increased vulnerability to drug and alcohol abuse.

CMHC also suggests three steps to improve self-esteem. Briefly these are:

1. Rebut the Inner Critic
2. Practice Self Compassion
3. Get Help from Others

We shall take a closer at these steps in detail later in the book. For now let's examine what the result of too much self-esteem can be.

Kids with higher self-esteem are more likely to engage in risk-taking behaviors. People with excessive self-esteem also tend to have worse relationships because they blame their partners for any problems with the relationship, they tend to see others as inferior. Excessive self-esteem is also linked to a higher frequency of violent and aggressive behaviors.

That isn't to suggest that self-esteem and confidence are bad things. In some situations, even excessive self-confidence can actually lead to some success. Highly self-confident people can sometimes bluff their way through situations, convincing others that they truly have the abilities behind their inflated sense of self.

In other cases, excess confidence can be seen as deceit or even narcissism, qualities that might make an employee less appealing to current and future employers.

Overconfidence in our own abilities is something that happens to everyone once in a while. You might over-estimate your ability to finish a project by a certain date, only to run out of time before the project is due. The good thing is that such overconfidence is often self-correcting.

Just a few instances of turning in late or shoddy work is probably enough to make you take a serious look at your time management skills. The next time a project is due, you are more likely to manage your time wisely and be more realistic about how long it will take you to complete the work.

If this overconfidence becomes habitual you can risk taking on more than you can chew too often and create uncomfortable consequences.

More Self-Esteem Improvement

V *anessa had to go and do some shopping to pre-pare an evening meal for her family. She was feeling low because she had neglected to have dental work done. On her way to the corner store she came across her friend who was just returning from the store. Vanessa noticed her friend was wearing a bright new frock and said to her "Wow, what a lovely frock you're wearing, it fits you so well and you look so good in it.*

In her book *The 10 Best Ever Depression Management Techniques*, Margaret Wehrenberg suggests that not-ing what is good or pleasing in others and compliment-ing on them has the double effect of not only boosting the other person's self-esteem, but also yours. Why not try doing this yourself?

When you notice something good or pleasing in other people, let them know, compliment them. This will not only make them feel good but it will make them feel good too.

AFFIRMATIONS

There is a lot to say about affirmations when they are done properly. They say it is not possible to hold both a positive and a negative though in your mind in the same moment.

I have successfully used affirmations for clients in my practice many times. The key to successful affirmation is to interrupt your unwanted, unpleasant thought. Once this thought is interrupted it creates a gap. Fill in the gap with something pleasant, this creates a positive mental 'environment' in which to place the affirmation.

I am going to share with you the exact technique that I successfully used many times in my clinic using one of the examples previously given:

1. Close your eyes and bring up the unwanted thought - e.g. "*I'll never get out of debt*"

2. Now imagine a STOP sign (like you see at some intersections) pop up where the thought is and say to yourself loudly in your mind "***STOP!***" In an authoritative voice.

3. Replace the image of the stop sign with a pleasant scene of your choice e.g. A beautiful beach with soft white sand, the gentle sound of waves

lapping at the shore, the seagulls gliding in the distance, bright blue sky above.

4. Once you are feeling good in this scene bring in your affirmation in a gentle but strong authoritative voice - *"I manage my money better so that I become debt free"*

5. Repeat it over and over, at least seven times.

6. Do this repeatedly for 7 days, take a break for 2 days then repeat the whole pattern another 2 times.

REMEMBER THAT YOU ARE CREATING A NEW NEURAL PATHWAY (CONNECTION IN THE BRAIN) TO OVERRIDE AN OLD UNWANTED PATHWAY. YOU ARE INSTALLING A NEW, BENEFICIAL THINKING HABIT - IT HAS BEEN SHOWN THAT IT TAKES AT LEAST 21 DAYS TO CREATE A NEW HABIT.

So here is a summary of the technique:

Old thought > STOP > Pleasant scene > Affirmation, 7 repetitions - do for 21 days.

About twenty five years ago a girlfriend took up with another man that popped up from her past leaving me hurt, devastated and in a low state of self-esteem.

This is a very personal story but it is a very good example that you can follow if ever you are in the same situation. What did I do to recover my self-esteem?

At the time I was using my van to do some deliveries as a way to earn extra income to support my hypnotherapy practice. I had a portable tape player in the van so while I was on my delivery runs I played tapes of music that took me back to the times when I had people around me that liked me and made me feel appreciated. I played them LOUD! The memories of those times flooded back filling me with good feelings. I revelled in the good feelings and let them saturate every part of me. It restored my self-esteem and self appreciation.

<u>In summary this is the technique you can use in similar circumstances:</u>

Feeling low self-esteem > Use something (e.g. music from a time you felt good about yourself) > Remember and revel in the good feelings, let them saturate every part of you > self-esteem and self appreciation will return!

<u>Seeing the other side of the issue:</u>

Elaine asked me *"How do I regain my self-esteem after my husband left me because of my illness and constant complaining about my pain?"*

My answer was simple *"The problem is not with you, you are bravely suffering your disease. Your husband's inability to cope with your discomfort is the problem."*

<u>Another technique - Goal setting</u>

Use this technique with caution because it could backfire. It has been proved from personal experience and the experience reported by others that low self-esteem often comes about because of lack of achievement.

This is where goal setting comes in, being cautious that you are realistic about the goal that you set. Be sure you know your goal is achievable. If you set a goal that is too high and fail to achieve it, it will set your self-esteem back. Let me use a simple example.

Your room is very untidy, you have a pile of worn clothes in one corner, books on the floor and your bedside cabinet is a mess of used tissues, empty coffee cups, empty pill bottles and dust. You feel bad about yourself living in this mess so you decide to do something about it but at the same time you feel overwhelmed by the mess and feel powerless to do anything about it.

I have personally experienced this and known others who have gone through the same experience. This is how I dealt with it, then passed the technique to a friend who was having a similar issue:

Knowing that the thought of cleaning and tidying the whole room would be an overwhelming task I avoided setting myself the goal altogether. What I did instead was to set the goal to clean and tidy one corner of the room at a time, and not necessarily all corners in the one day.

The dynamics behind using this technique are:

1. You achieve the goal of cleaning and tidying one quarter of the room easily.
2. Achieving that goal will make you feel satisfied and better about yourself.
3. Knowing that you have cleaned and tidied one quarter of the room will motivate you to do the same in the next quarter of the room though not necessarily on the same day.
4. Once you have done the whole room you will feel so much better about yourself and will be motivated to move on to another task.

EXERCISE AND NUTRITION AS A BOOST TO SELF-ESTEEM

Never overlook the benefits of exercise. A good workout that raises your endorphin level and will make you feel good about yourself. When you exercise regularly and eat healthy foods you feel better naturally.

Self-Esteem and Drug and Alcohol Abuse

J osh was so happy when his daughter Adele was born; she meant the world to him. Josh's ambition when I first met him years before was to marry and have children, and he wanted his children to be his friends.

You wouldn't know when speaking to Josh, that he had a short fuse temper because he was so polite and well mannered. The temper was the source of his troubles. He had grown up holding old fashioned values, and he brought these into his marriage. It turned out that his wife did not have the same values. Where he expected that she would clean, cook and be there for him, the wife was different. She had a full time job and would often join her work colleagues for drinks after work. This infuriated Josh and they often had heated confrontations.

The end result was that he was served with an AVO. His wife filed for divorce against him and won. Josh fought for custody of Adele but he lost the battle and was also forbidden from visiting her.*

Josh keeps in touch with me through Facebook Messenger, he is very depressed and told me that the only thing that would make him feel better was to see his daughter. The last time he got in touch he told me he was living in his car. I asked him *"What have you done to get you there?"* His answer was *"Don't judge me Alfred, I've been using heroin."* The issue is a lot more complicated and many other factors were involved but self-esteem was definitely affected.

I had tried in the past to help Josh, listened to him when he was going through bad times, trying to guide him in the right direction. Then I lost touch with him after I retired and moved away. It never occured to me that his self-esteem had been at risk. I knew he smoked pot from time to time but it came as a surprise to me that he started to use heroin.

Another case; About a year ago, a friend came up from Sydney with one of his friends whom I shall call Danny.

---

* An **AVO** is an Apprehended Violence Order. It is an order to protect victims of domestic violence when they are fearful of future violence or threats to their safety. They are sometimes called restraining orders or protection orders.

Danny was a very likeable guy but he liked to drink all the time. I rarely saw him sober. He told me his wife threw him out of home. According to his story, his wife belittled him because she wanted a child and claimed he wasn't man enough and was impotent because she didn't conceive. The fact that he had two daughters from a previous marriage didn't seem enough evidence that he wasn't impotent and when he brought that up it made her more angry.

I could understand how his wife's belittlement would have affected his self-esteem, he still loved her and wanted to be with her and was deeply hurt, the drinking helped "drown his sorrows," as they say.

These two cases are just examples of how drug and alcohol abuse can go hand in hand with low self-esteem. Of course the problem runs deeper than that and other factors are involved, but this is not a book about drug and alcohol abuse. Perhaps it will become the topic for another book.

Then there is the addiction to food, like Nathan who is overweight. Nathan doesn't eat just because he is hungry, he eats because he doesn't feel good about himself too. Nathan has invited me to eat with him a few times. My eating habits are different, I am happy with a run of the mill hamburger or pizza. Not Nathan, he has to go to a proper restaurant and order extravagantly, it almost makes me feel guilty for his spending, but he doesn't seem to care, it makes him feel good.

Many people turn to alcohol or drugs or excessive eating because they either feel bad about themselves or the circumstances around them, or their inability to cope with circumstances. In any case, low self-esteem is usually a factor. Maybe you know people who need to 'have a couple of drinks or a couple of 'bongs' or a snort of cocaine before they go out somewhere. Usually it's to work up enough confidence to socialize or to add to their enjoyment.

What You Have Learned from this Book and More

The first few chapters gave you a good explanation of the general concept of self-esteem and all its components. You were also given some tools to evaluate your own self-esteem overall and the opportunity to analyse different aspects of it so that you know exactly where you stand. Knowing more about self-esteem places you in a better position to repair and improve it because it's easier to deal with the devil you know than the devil you don't know.

You learned what can happen when you have too little or too much self-esteem and you were introduced to the concept of your inner critic, how to discover your inner critic and how to convert your inner critic into an ally. You were also given some examples and exercises on how you can do this

As you got deeper into the book you learned about your values and what role they can play in the development of your self-esteem. Again you were given examples and exercises through which you can make adjustments if your values are interfering with your self-esteem.

The same with core beliefs, you learned how they develop and were given examples and exercises on how you could adjust your core beliefs so they could serve you better.

To deal with the question of how you repair self-esteem in victims of abuse or neglect I dedicated a whole chapter that introduces reframing and which leads into explanation of the Inner Child concept and a technique on healing this child within.

Further along more techniques were given that help with repair and improvement of self-esteem and a response was given for parents who had asked me how to bring up children so that they develop a healthy self-esteem.

Finally you were given some examples how self-esteem could be linked with drug and alcohol abuse and overeating.

Now here are some more suggestions on How to have healthy self-esteem. These come from National Health Service of UK:

To boost your self-esteem, you need to identify the negative beliefs you have about yourself, then challenge them.

You may tell yourself you're "too stupid" to apply for a new job, for example, or that "nobody cares" about you.

Start to note these negative thoughts and write them on a piece of paper or in a diary. Ask yourself when you first started to think these thoughts.

Next, start to write some evidence that challenges these negative beliefs, such as, "I'm really good at cryptic crosswords" or "My sister calls for a chat every week".

Write down other positive things about yourself, such as "I'm thoughtful" or "I'm a great cook" or "I'm someone that others trust".

Also write some good things that other people say about you.

Aim to have at least 5 positive things on your list and add to it regularly. Then put your list somewhere you can see it. That way, you can keep reminding yourself that you're OK.

You might have low confidence now because of what happened when you were growing up, but we can grow and develop new ways of seeing ourselves at any age.

Other ways to improve low self-esteem

Here are some other simple techniques that may help you feel better about yourself.

Recognise what you're good at

We're all good at something, whether it's cooking, singing, doing puzzles or being a friend. We also tend to enjoy doing the things we're good at, which can help boost your mood.

Build positive relationships

If you find certain people tend to bring you down, try to spend less time with them, or tell them how you feel about their words or actions.

Try to build relationships with people who are positive and who appreciate you.

Be kind to yourself

Being kind to yourself means being gentle to yourself at times when you feel like being self-critical.

Think what you'd say to a friend in a similar situation. We often give far better advice to others than we do to ourselves.

Learn to be assertive

Being assertive is about respecting other people's opinions and needs, and expecting the same from them.

One trick is to look at other people who act assertively and copy what they do.

It's not about pretending you're someone you're not. It's picking up hints and tips from people you admire and letting the real you come out.

Start saying "no"

People with low self-esteem often feel they have to say yes to other people, even when they do not really want to.

The risk is that you become overburdened, resentful, angry and depressed.

For the most part, saying no does not upset relationships. It can be helpful to keep saying no, but in different ways, until they get the message.

Give yourself a challenge

We all feel nervous or afraid to do things at times. But people with healthy self-esteem do not let these feelings stop them trying new things or taking on challenges.

Set yourself a goal, such as joining an exercise class or going to a social occasion. Achieving your goals will help to increase your self-esteem.

If you really need outside help seek some counseling or other kind of therapy from a licensed professional.

What to Do Now

Y ou are reading this and you can breathe in and out comfortably, and your unconscious mind can absorb and apply all the learnings and information given in this book.

Remember that you are a unique human being and whatever you think or feel about yourself is not always the real you. You still have time to discover and celebrate who you really are.

Flaws in self-esteem do not happen overnight except as result of some extreme event so they could take some time to heal. The information and exercises in this book will have helped to increase your self-esteem and you can take this further.

You can read the whole book again or select relevant sections to reinforce what you have learned. You can repeat the exercises if you need. Better still be creative and invent exercises that deal directly with your own issues. The examples you were given should serve as a good platform from which to do this.

- Repair the damage that was caused to your self-esteem
- Discover who YOU really are
- Become the YOU that you were really destined to be
- You can do it!

Other Books by this Author

- Depression Self Help: How to break through depression
- Anxiety Self Help: How to overcome anxiety

Recommended Reading

Doidge, Norman - "The Brain That Changes Itself," Scribe Publications, 1 March 2010

Hadley, Josie and Carol Staudacher. "Hypnosis for Change" - New Harbinger Publications Inc

McKay, Matthew and Patrick Fanning "Self-Esteem:" New Harbinger Publications Inc.

Wehrenberg, Margaret. "The 10 Best-Ever Depression Management Techniques" - W.W.Norton & Company. New York, London

Yapko, Michael "Breaking the Patterns of Depression" Broadway Books New York

References

Newsome, Teresa. "Signs You Have Low Self-Esteem in a Relationship." *bustle.com*, 11 May 2016. Web 9 Sept 2020

"Self-Esteem." *betterhealthvic.gov.au*, Better Health Channel. Web 9 Sept 2020

Adler, Nancy and Judith Stewart. "Self-Esteem" MacArthur Research Network on SES.& Health, *macses.ucsf.edu*, University of California, March 2004, Web 9 Sept. 2020

"Do You Know the 3 Types of Self-Esteem" *exploringyourmind.com*, Psychology, 24 Nov 2016, Web 9 Sept 2020

"Self-Esteem: What Is It?" Dept of Sociology. *Socy. umd.edu*, University of Maryland, 2 Aug 2019, Web 9 Sept 2020

Rosenberg, M. (1965). "Society and the adolescent self-image." *fetzer.org*, Princeton, NJ: Princeton University Press. Web 9 Sept 2020

Frankl, Viktor. "Man's Search for Meaning" *en.wikipedia. org*, Originally published 1946, Web 9 Sept 2020

"Self-Esteem" en.wikipedia.org, 31 Aug 2020, Web 9 Sept 2020

Self-Esteem Second Edition Matthew McKay PhD & Patrick Fanning – New Harbinger Publications Inc

"Self-Esteem in Children." Pregnancy Birth & Baby. *pregnancybirthbaby.org.au*, May 2019. Web. 9 Sept 2020

"Building Self-Esteem: Babies and Children" *raising-children.net.au*, Australian Government Department of Social Services, 7 July 2017, Web 9 Sept 2020

Conti, Vicki. "Gene Linked to Optimism and Self Esteem." *nih.gov/news-events,* National Institute of Health, 26 Sept 2011, Web 9 Sept 2020

"Student Confidence and Self-Esteem." edu-nova.com/articles, Web 9 Sept 2020

Hadley, Josie and Carol Staudacher. "Hypnosis for Change" Second Edition - New Harbinger Publications Inc

Branden, Nathaniel "The Six Pillars of Self Esteem." Bantam Books, June 1995

"Self Esteem." *cmch.utexas.edu*, The University of Texas at Austin Counseling and Mental Health Centre, Web 9 Sept 2020

Cherry, Kendra. "When Too Much Self-Confidence is a Bad Thing." *verywellmind.com*, 28 July 2019, Web 9 Sept 2020

"Value (Ethics)" *en.wikipedia.com*, 7 Aug 2020, Web 9 Sept 2020

Brandt, Andrea, "9 Steps to Healing Childhood Trauma as an Adult" *psychologytoday.com*, 2 April 2018, Web 9 Sept 2020

Rossi, Ernest. "Micro-array Analysis of DNA After Hypnotherapy and Counseling" Sept 2008, Journal of Clinical Hypnosis and Hypnotherapy, The Australian Society of Clinical Hypnotherapy

Shorten, Andrew "How to Identify Core Beliefs That Control Your Life" *thelawofattraction.com,* Web 9 Sept 2020

Beating Drug Addiction - The Rat Park Experiment - youtube.com

Discipline in Montessori - With Miss Donna (Part 2) - youtube.com

"Self-Esteem and Teenagers" *reachout.com*, Web 9 Sept 20

Rigby, Ken and Ian Cox "The Contribution of Bullying at School and Low Self-Esteem to Acts of Delinquency Among Australian Teenagers" *sciencedirect.com*, Elsevier Science

D'Arcy, Lyness - Reviewer. "How Can I Improve My Self-Esteem," kidshealth.org" from Nemours, Aug 2018, Web 9 Sept 2020

Doidge, Norman - "The Brain That Changes Itself," Scribe Publications, 1 March 2010

Wehrenberg, Margaret - The 10 Best Ever Depression Management Techniques, W.W. Norton & Company, New York. London